Financial Odyssey

Navigating Wealth and Wisdom

Manoj Sam & Jay Kumar

ISBN: 978-1-73237-409-6

Published by
INDUS NETWORK
Fort Myers, Florida 33913

सुपथा विश्वा अर्या निः संदृशते यत्त्वया जुष्टम यज्ञम् ।
तन्नो अस्तु दीव्यत्तमं वयं स्याम पतये रयिम् ।।

Rigveda (10.191.1).

Transliteration

supathā viśvā aryā niḥ saṁdṛśate yat tvayā juṣṭam yajñam
tanno astu dīvyattamaṁ vayaṁ syāma pataye rayim

Translation

O noble one, the path of prosperity shown

by you is indeed praiseworthy.

May we be blessed with divine wealth

by performing the rituals according to your guidance.

Foreword

Welcome to "Financial Odyssey - Navigating Wealth and Wisdom," a captivating journey through the realms of financial literacy, personal growth, and the pursuit of financial independence. In these pages, you will accompany Alex, a relatable protagonist navigating the complexities of money management, guided by mentors, stories, and practical lessons.

In our modern world, financial literacy is more than just a skill; it's a gateway to empowerment and freedom. The stories woven into this book offer not only insights into financial principles but also a narrative of resilience, determination, and the transformative power of knowledge.

From the stark realities of economic downturns to the inspiring tales of entrepreneurial success, each chapter illuminates crucial aspects of financial life. Through encounters with mentors like Mr. Leonard and Ms. Martinez, Alex discovers that wealth isn't merely about earning money but understanding how to make it work for you.

As Alex progresses from uncertainty to confidence, facing challenges such as unexpected medical bills and the weight of student loans, we witness a transformation fueled by practical strategies and unwavering perseverance. The journey culminates in a profound realization: that financial security is within reach for anyone willing to embark on the path of learning and disciplined action.

This book is not just about financial success; it's a call to action for every reader to take control of their financial future. Whether you are a recent graduate like Alex or someone seeking to enhance your financial acumen, the lessons here will resonate deeply. Through reflection, education, and practical application, you too can chart a course towards financial mastery and create a legacy of stability and prosperity.

Join Alex and embark on this odyssey of discovery. May it inspire you to embrace your financial journey with courage, wisdom, and a commitment to lifelong learning.

Chapter

Chapter 1

A Call to Adventure

Alex stood at the threshold of a new chapter, heart brimming with excitement and a touch of trepidation. Clutching a freshly printed degree, they stepped into the bustling world beyond the university gates. The sky seemed to stretch endlessly, echoing the boundless possibilities that lay ahead. A recent college graduate, Alex was ready to embark on a journey of professional growth and self-discovery. But amidst the thrill of new beginnings, a nagging uncertainty loomed in the back of their mind: the daunting task of managing personal finances.

Alex had always been a diligent student, excelling in academics and extracurricular activities. However, financial literacy had never been a part of their formal education. Growing up, money was a topic rarely discussed at home, and Alex often found themselves in a haze of confusion when it came to budgeting, saving, and investing. As graduation day approached, the excitement of landing a promising job offer was tempered by the realization that financial independence required more than just a steady paycheck.

One sunny afternoon, a conversation with a mentor would become the catalyst for Alex's awakening to the importance of financial literacy. Dr. Harper, a seasoned professor and advisor, had been a guiding light throughout Alex's college years. Known for their wisdom and practical advice, Dr. Harper had an uncanny ability to make complex subjects approachable.

"Alex, congratulations on your graduation and the new job!" Dr. Harper exclaimed, a warm smile lighting up their face. "I remember the feeling of stepping into the world with a sense of purpose and excitement."

"Thank you, Dr. Harper. I'm really looking forward to starting this new chapter," Alex replied, trying to suppress the anxiety gnawing at them.

As if sensing the unspoken concern, Dr. Harper's expression softened. "Alex, you've worked hard to get here, and you should be proud. But I want to talk to you about something that's just as important as your career—your financial independence."

Alex's curiosity piqued. "Financial independence? I mean, I've thought about it, but I'm not really sure where to start."

Dr. Harper leaned back in their chair, thoughtful. "Let me tell you a story. When I graduated, I was just like you—eager to dive into my career but clueless about money. It wasn't until I hit a rough patch that I realized how critical financial literacy is. It's not just about earning money; it's about managing it wisely so you can build a secure and fulfilling life."

Alex listened intently, absorbing every word. Dr. Harper continued, "Think of financial independence as an adventure. Just like any journey, it requires planning, knowledge, and the willingness to learn from experiences. It starts with understanding your income, expenses, and savings. But it's more than that—it's about setting goals, making informed decisions, and building habits that will serve you throughout your life."

The conversation stretched on, covering topics from budgeting basics to the power of compound interest. Dr. Harper shared personal anecdotes and practical tips, turning what once seemed like an intimidating subject into an engaging discussion.

As the sun dipped below the horizon, painting the sky in hues of orange and pink, Alex felt a newfound sense of clarity and determination. They realized that the journey to financial independence wasn't a solitary endeavor. With the guidance of mentors like Dr. Harper and a willingness to learn, they could navigate the complexities of personal finance.

That evening, Alex returned to their apartment, head buzzing with ideas and a resolve to take charge of their financial future. The conversation with Dr. Harper had ignited a spark—a call to adventure. Alex knew that this journey would have its challenges, but it was a journey worth embarking on. For the first time, they felt empowered to transform their dreams into reality, one financial decision at a time.

And so, with a heart full of hope and a mind brimming with newfound knowledge, Alex took the first step on the path to financial independence. The adventure had begun.

A Call to Adventure

1. **Financial Literacy is Essential**:
   - Financial independence requires more than just earning a steady paycheck.
   - Understanding personal finances is crucial for building a secure and fulfilling life.
2. **Importance of Guidance and Mentorship**:
   - Mentors, like Dr. Harper, provide invaluable wisdom and practical advice.
   - Guidance from experienced individuals can make complex subjects more approachable.
3. **Planning and Knowledge**:
   - Financial independence is a journey that requires careful planning and continuous learning.
   - Key components include understanding income, expenses, and savings.
4. **Budgeting Basics**:
   - Budgeting is fundamental to managing money wisely.
   - Knowing where your money goes helps in making informed financial decisions.

5. **Setting Financial Goals**:

    - Establishing clear, achievable financial goals is essential.

    - Goals provide direction and motivation for financial planning.

6. **Compound Interest**:

    - The power of compound interest is significant in wealth accumulation.

    - Starting early with savings and investments maximizes the benefits of compounding.

7. **Informed Decision-Making**:

    - Making informed financial decisions is key to long-term stability.

    - Continuous education and staying informed about financial matters is crucial.

8. **Building Positive Financial Habits**:

    - Developing and maintaining good financial habits is vital for financial independence.

    - Consistent saving, prudent spending, and wise investing are part of these habits.

9. **Embracing the Financial Journey**:

    - Financial independence is an ongoing adventure with its own challenges.

- Viewing it as a journey makes the process engaging and rewarding.

10. **Empowerment Through Financial Education**:

    - Financial education empowers individuals to take control of their financial futures.
    - Knowledge and preparation build confidence in managing personal finances.

11. **Taking the First Step**:

    - The journey to financial independence begins with a single step.
    - Being proactive and starting the process is crucial for long-term success.

12. **Resilience and Adaptability**:

    - The journey will have challenges, but resilience and a willingness to learn from experiences are essential.
    - Adapting to new financial knowledge and circumstances ensures progress.

13. **Transforming Dreams into Reality**:

    - Financial planning and literacy help in turning dreams into achievable goals.
    - Each financial decision contributes to building a secure and prosperous future.

Chapter 2

Reflections on Two Decades

It was a crisp autumn day when Alex met Sarah at a financial literacy conference. The event was bustling with attendees from various backgrounds, all eager to learn and share their experiences. During a break between sessions, Alex found a quiet corner and struck up a conversation with Sarah, a woman in her early thirties with a thoughtful expression and a determined demeanor.

As they exchanged pleasantries, the topic of conversation naturally drifted to personal financial journeys. Sarah mentioned that her perspective on money had been profoundly shaped by the 2008 financial crisis.

"I was just a teenager then," Sarah began, her voice tinged with a mix of nostalgia and lingering sadness. "My parents lost our home due to mortgage issues. It was a tough time for us, and it left a lasting impact on how I view financial stability."

Alex listened intently as Sarah recounted her story. In 2008, Sarah's family lived in a modest suburban home. Her father worked in construction, and her mother was a part-time teacher. They were a typical middle-class family, working hard to provide a stable life for their children. However, the financial storm that year changed everything.

"I remember the day my parents sat me down to explain what was happening," Sarah said, her eyes distant as she recalled the moment. "They told me that we couldn't keep up with the mortgage payments and that we might lose the house. It was terrifying. Our home wasn't just a building; it was where we felt safe and secure."

Sarah described how the crisis had affected her family. Her father's work in construction had dried up as the housing market collapsed, and her mother's part-time income wasn't enough to cover the mounting bills. Despite their best efforts, the day came when they had to leave their home.

"Packing up our belongings and moving to a small apartment was one of the hardest things I've ever experienced," Sarah admitted. "But it also taught me valuable lessons about resilience and the importance of financial literacy."

Sarah's story resonated deeply with Alex. The 2008 financial crisis had been a wake-up call for many, highlighting the fragility of financial stability and the importance of being prepared for the unexpected.

"How did that experience shape your approach to finances?" Alex asked, genuinely curious.

"It made me realize that financial stability isn't just about having a steady income," Sarah explained. "It's about understanding the bigger picture—knowing how to manage debt, save for emergencies, and make informed decisions about money."

She went on to describe how she had dedicated herself to learning about personal finance. "I started reading books, attending workshops, and seeking advice from anyone willing to share their knowledge. I wanted to make sure I never found myself in a situation like that again."

Sarah's determination paid off. She managed to save diligently, invest wisely, and build a solid financial foundation. Over the years, she had also become an advocate for financial literacy, helping others understand the importance of financial planning and resilience.

Alex and Sarah continued to discuss the broader impact of the 2008 financial crisis. They talked about how it had exposed systemic issues in the financial industry and led to significant changes in regulations and policies. The crisis had also sparked a greater awareness of the need for financial education and the importance of preparing for economic downturns.

"The crisis showed us that financial stability is more than just a personal responsibility," Sarah said. "It's also about the systems and structures in place that support or undermine that stability. We need to advocate for policies that protect consumers and promote financial literacy at all levels."

As the conversation ended, Alex felt a deep sense of admiration for Sarah's resilience and determination. Her story was a powerful reminder of the importance of financial literacy and the impact that unexpected events can have on our lives.

"Thank you for sharing your story, Sarah," Alex said sincerely. "It's inspiring to see how you've turned a challenging experience into a source of strength and motivation."

Sarah smiled warmly. "And thank you, Alex. It's conversations like these that remind me of the importance of community and shared learning. We're all in this together, and by sharing our experiences, we can help each other grow."

Leaving the conference, Alex reflected on the profound lessons learned from Sarah's story. The 2008 financial crisis had been a pivotal moment for many, shaping their understanding of financial stability and highlighting the importance of preparedness.

For Alex, the conversation reinforced the belief that financial education and resilience were crucial for building a secure future. It also underscored the importance of community and support in navigating financial challenges.

As Alex continued on their own financial journey, they felt a renewed sense of purpose. The journey was not just about personal success but also about helping others achieve financial stability and security. Inspired by Sarah's story, Alex resolved to keep advocating for financial literacy and supporting those on their own financial journeys.

The adventure of financial growth and learning was ongoing, filled with new challenges and opportunities. With each step, Alex was not only building their own financial future but also contributing to a larger movement of financial empowerment and resilience.

Reflections on Two Decades

1. **Impact of the 2008 Financial Crisis**:

   - The crisis had a profound impact on many families, including Sarah's, who lost their home due to mortgage issues.

   - Highlighted the fragility of financial stability and the importance of being prepared for unexpected events.

2. **Personal Financial Journey**:

   - Sarah's experience shaped her understanding of financial stability, emphasizing the need for comprehensive financial literacy.

   - Financial stability goes beyond having a steady income; it involves managing debt, saving for emergencies, and making informed financial decisions.

3. **Resilience and Financial Literacy**:

    - The crisis taught Sarah valuable lessons about resilience and the importance of financial education.

    - Sarah dedicated herself to learning about personal finance through books, workshops, and seeking advice.

4. **Building a Solid Financial Foundation**:

    - Sarah managed to save diligently, invest wisely, and build a robust financial foundation.

    - She became an advocate for financial literacy, helping others understand financial planning and resilience.

5. **Systemic Issues and Policy Changes**:

    - The 2008 crisis exposed systemic issues in the financial industry, leading to significant changes in regulations and policies.

    - Sparked greater awareness of the need for financial education and preparing for economic downturns.

6. **Advocacy for Financial Literacy**:

    - Financial stability involves both personal responsibility and supportive systems and structures.

    - Advocating for policies that protect consumers and promote financial literacy at all levels is essential.

7. **Community and Shared Learning**:

   - The importance of community and shared learning in navigating financial challenges.
   - Conversations and sharing experiences can help individuals grow and support each other.

8. **Continuous Financial Education**:

   - The conversation with Sarah reinforced the belief in the importance of ongoing financial education and resilience.
   - Building a secure future requires continuous learning and adaptability.

9. **Helping Others Achieve Financial Stability**:

   - The journey is not just about personal success but also about helping others achieve financial stability and security.
   - Inspired by Sarah's story, Alex resolved to advocate for financial literacy and support others on their financial journeys.

10. **Ongoing Financial Growth and Learning**:

   - The adventure of financial growth and learning is continuous, filled with new challenges and opportunities.
   - Each step contributes to building a secure financial future and promoting a larger movement of financial empowerment and resilience.

Chapter 3

The Secret of Wealth

On a crisp autumn morning, Alex took a leisurely stroll through the neighborhood, enjoying the vibrant tapestry of fall colors. It was a rare day off, and Alex was determined to make the most of it. As they walked past the elegant, ivy-clad house at the corner, they noticed an elderly man meticulously tending to his garden. The man was Mr. Leonard, a neighbor Alex had often seen but never really spoken to.

“Good morning, Mr. Leonard!” Alex called out, feeling a spontaneous burst of friendliness.

Mr. Leonard looked up from his roses, his face breaking into a warm, inviting smile. “Good morning! Beautiful day, isn’t it? Care to join me for some tea?”

Surprised but pleased by the invitation, Alex agreed. Moments later, they found themselves seated in Mr. Leonard’s cozy sunroom, sipping tea and admiring the well-kept garden.

"Alex, I've seen you around quite a bit. What keeps you busy these days?" Mr. Leonard asked, his eyes twinkling with genuine curiosity.

"I recently graduated and started my first job," Alex replied, feeling a mixture of pride and uncertainty. "It's exciting, but managing finances is challenging. I'm trying to learn as much as I can about saving and investing."

Mr. Leonard nodded thoughtfully. "Ah, the beginning of your journey. I remember those days well. But let me tell you a little secret about wealth—it's not just about how much you earn, but how well you manage and grow what you have."

Intrigued, Alex leaned in closer. "I've heard you're quite successful, Mr. Leonard. But I rarely see you working long hours like many others. How do you do it?"

With a chuckle, Mr. Leonard set down his teacup and began to share his story. "It's true, I don't follow the conventional path. When I was younger, I worked hard like everyone else, but I soon realized that wealth isn't built solely on the back of labor. It's built on the foundation of smart investments and understanding the flow of money."

He continued, "In my thirties, I started investing in stocks, real estate, and bonds. I learned to analyze market trends and diversify my portfolio. It wasn't about getting rich quick, but about making informed decisions and being patient."

Alex listened intently, absorbing every word. "So, you don't have to work long hours to be wealthy?"

"Exactly," Mr. Leonard said, his eyes gleaming with wisdom. "The key is to let your money work for you. I spend my days managing my investments, but it's not a full-time job. It's about having a strategy and sticking to it, even when the market is unpredictable."

He leaned back in his chair, a look of contentment on his face. "Once my investments began to generate passive income, I had more time to enjoy life. I travel, tend to my garden, and pursue hobbies I love. Financial independence gave me the freedom to live life on my terms."

Alex felt a surge of inspiration. "How can someone like me start on this path?"

Mr. Leonard smiled kindly. "Start by educating yourself. There are countless resources—books, courses, and mentors. Understand the basics of investing, learn to budget, and live within your means. The earlier you start, the more time your money has to grow."

He paused, looking thoughtfully at Alex. "But remember, wealth isn't just about money. It's about having the time and freedom to do what you love. It's about security and peace of mind. Chase those, and the money will follow."

The conversation stretched into the afternoon, with Mr. Leonard sharing tips and stories from his decades of experience. By the time Alex left, they felt a renewed sense of purpose and a clearer vision of their financial journey.

As Alex walked home, they reflected on Mr. Leonard's words. The secret of wealth wasn't hidden in the endless grind of long hours, but in the smart, strategic management of resources. It was about letting money work for you and finding balance and fulfillment in life.

That day marked a turning point for Alex. They resolved to educate themselves about investing, to seek out opportunities for passive income, and to build a life that wasn't solely defined by work. With Mr. Leonard's wisdom as a guiding light, Alex felt ready to embark on this new adventure towards financial independence and true wealth.

The Secret of Wealth

1. Wealth Management Over Hard Work:

   - Wealth is not solely built through hard work but through smart management and growth of resources.

   - Effective wealth creation involves strategic investments and understanding the flow of money.

2. Smart Investments:

   - Diversify investments across stocks, real estate, and bonds.

   - Analyze market trends and make informed decisions rather than seeking quick riches.

- Be patient and consistent with investment strategies.

3. **Passive Income**:

   - Aim to generate passive income through investments to achieve financial independence.

   - Passive income allows for more free time to enjoy life and pursue personal interests.

4. **Financial Strategy**:

   - Develop and stick to a financial strategy, even when the market is unpredictable.

   - Educate yourself continuously about investing, budgeting, and financial management.

5. **Early Start and Consistency**:

   - Start financial planning and investing early to give money more time to grow.

   - Live within your means and focus on long-term financial goals.

6. **Financial Independence**:

   - Financial independence provides the freedom to live life on your own terms.

   - Wealth is about having time, freedom, security, and peace of mind.

7. **Continuous Learning**:

- Utilize various resources such as books, courses, and mentors to enhance financial knowledge.
- Seek opportunities to learn and grow financially continuously.

8. **Balanced Life**:

- Wealth should not solely define life; find balance and fulfillment through personal interests and hobbies.
- Achieving financial goals should enhance overall quality of life, not detract from it.

9. **Inspiration and Guidance**:

- Mentors and experienced individuals can provide valuable insights and guidance on the path to financial independence.
- Learning from others' experiences can help shape your financial journey effectively.

10. **Renewed Purpose**:

- Embrace a clear vision and purpose for financial growth and independence.
- Use newfound knowledge and inspiration to embark on a journey toward financial freedom and a fulfilling life.

Chapter 4

The Power of Knowledge

Alex had always been keen on self-improvement, and the flyer for a community workshop on financial literacy seemed like the perfect opportunity to gain some much-needed knowledge. The workshop, titled "Empowering Your Financial Future," promised to cover essential topics such as budgeting, investing, and debt management. As Alex entered the community center, they noticed the room buzzing with anticipation. People of all ages and backgrounds filled the seats, each with their own reasons for being there.

At the front of the room stood Ms. Martinez, a dynamic and passionate financial educator known for her engaging teaching style. With a warm smile and an air of confidence, she welcomed everyone and began the session.

“Good evening, everyone! I’m delighted to see so many of you here. Tonight, we’re going to talk about something that can change your life: financial literacy."

Alex listened attentively as Ms. Martinez explained the basics of budgeting, the importance of saving, and the fundamentals of investing. Her enthusiasm was infectious, and her ability to break down complex concepts into simple, relatable terms made the information accessible to all.

"Financial literacy is more than just understanding numbers," Ms. Martinez said, her voice filled with conviction. "It's about empowerment. When you understand how money works, you can make informed decisions that improve your life and the lives of those around you."

She shared stories of people who had fallen into financial traps due to a lack of knowledge. There was the young couple who took on an adjustable-rate mortgage without understanding the risks, and the single mother who struggled with high-interest credit card debt because she didn't know about better borrowing options.

"These stories aren't meant to scare you," Ms. Martinez explained. "They're meant to illustrate the pitfalls of financial ignorance. But the good news is, with knowledge, you can avoid these traps and build a secure future."

Alex felt a mix of emotions—sympathy for those who had struggled, and a growing determination to avoid similar mistakes. Ms. Martinez's words resonated deeply, especially her emphasis on the transformative power of education.

"Let's talk about investing," Ms. Martinez continued. "Many people think investing is only for the wealthy, but that's a myth.

Anyone can start investing with the right knowledge and strategy. The key is to start early and be consistent."

She introduced the concept of compound interest, illustrating how small, regular investments could grow significantly over time. Alex was fascinated by the idea that their money could work for them, growing steadily and creating a foundation for financial stability.

During a break, Alex approached Ms. Martinez with a burning question. "Ms. Martinez, how do you stay motivated to keep learning about finance? It can seem overwhelming at times."

Ms. Martinez smiled warmly. "I understand, Alex. It can be overwhelming but think of it as an ongoing journey. Start with the basics, and as you grow more comfortable, delve into more complex topics. Remember, every bit of knowledge you gain empowers you to make better decisions. Set small goals, celebrate your progress, and keep pushing forward."

As the workshop continued, Alex found themselves inspired not only by the information but by Ms. Martinez's passion and dedication. The session concluded with a Q&A, and Alex felt a renewed sense of confidence as they listened to others' questions and Ms. Martinez's thoughtful answers.

Before leaving, Ms. Martinez shared one final piece of advice. "Financial literacy isn't just about securing your future; it's about creating opportunities. It's about giving you the freedom to pursue your dreams without the constant worry of financial instability. Knowledge is power, and with it, you can build the life you envision."

Walking out of the community center, Alex felt a profound sense of empowerment. The workshop had opened their eyes to the importance of financial literacy and the impact it could have on their life. They were no longer intimidated by the idea of managing money; instead, they were eager to apply what they had learned and continue their education.

Ms. Martinez's words echoed in Alex's mind as they made their way home. Financial literacy was indeed a powerful tool, and Alex was determined to wield it wisely. The journey ahead might be challenging but armed with knowledge and a newfound sense of purpose, Alex felt ready to take control of their financial future.

The Power of Knowledge

1. **Importance of Financial Literacy**:
   - Financial literacy is more than just understanding numbers; it's about empowerment.
   - Knowing how money works enables informed decisions that improve lives.
2. **Fundamentals of Financial Management**:
   - Basics of budgeting, saving, and investing is essential.

- Understanding these fundamentals helps avoid financial traps.

3. **Pitfalls of Financial Ignorance**:

   - Lack of knowledge can lead to financial mistakes such as taking on high-risk mortgages or accumulating high-interest debt.

   - Awareness and education can prevent these pitfalls and build a secure future.

4. **Transformative Power of Education**:

   - Knowledge transforms lives by enabling better financial decisions.

   - Education is a continuous journey that builds confidence and financial stability.

5. **Investing for Everyone**:

   - Investing is not only for the wealthy; anyone can start with the right knowledge and strategy.

   - Start early and be consistent to benefit from compound interest and long-term growth.

6. **Ongoing Learning and Motivation**:

   - Financial education is an ongoing journey; start with basics and progress to more complex topics.

   - Set small goals, celebrate progress, and keep pushing forward.

7. **Creating Opportunities**:

- Financial literacy creates opportunities and gives the freedom to pursue dreams without financial instability.
- Knowledge empowers individuals to build the life they envision.

8. **Empowerment through Knowledge**:
    - Financial literacy empowers individuals, reducing intimidation around money management.
    - Continuous education and application of financial knowledge are key to taking control of one's financial future.
9. **Practical Advice from Mentors**:
    - Seek guidance from experienced mentors and educators.
    - Practical advice and real-life examples enhance understanding and application of financial concepts.
10. **Confidence and Purpose**:
    - Gaining financial knowledge instills confidence and a sense of purpose.
    - Empowerment through financial literacy leads to proactive management of finances and a secure future.

Chapter 5

Building Your Empire

A few months after attending the financial literacy workshop with Ms. Martinez, Alex found himself increasingly fascinated by the world of finance and business. He had always harbored a quiet dream of starting their own venture, and the workshop had ignited a spark of possibility. It was this newfound interest that led Alex to join a local startup incubator, a vibrant hub for budding entrepreneurs looking to turn their ideas into successful businesses.

The incubator, located in a sleek, modern building downtown, buzzed with energy and innovation. Entrepreneurs from various backgrounds and industries gathered there, each with their own unique vision and ambition. Alex felt both excited and slightly intimidated as they walked into the bustling space for the first time.

During the initial orientation session, Alex met Kate and Tom, two seasoned entrepreneurs who had transformed their small startups into thriving businesses. Kate, a dynamic and charismatic woman in her thirties, had founded an eco-friendly skincare company. Tom, a thoughtful and strategic thinker in his forties, had built a successful software development firm.

Over coffee breaks and collaborative sessions, Alex got to know Kate and Tom better, eager to learn from their experiences.

"Kate, how did you get started with your skincare business?" Alex asked one afternoon, genuinely curious about her journey.

Kate smiled, her eyes lighting up with enthusiasm. "It all began with a passion for natural beauty products and a desire to make a positive impact on the environment. I started making products in my kitchen, selling them at local farmers' markets. It was a slow start, but I believed in my vision."

She continued, "The turning point came when I joined this incubator. The mentorship, resources, and networking opportunities here were invaluable. I learned about branding, scaling operations, and securing funding. It wasn't easy, but taking those entrepreneurial risks paid off. Today, my products are in major retail stores and have a loyal customer base."

Tom nodded in agreement. "I had a similar experience. My background is in software development, and I saw a gap in the market for customizable business solutions. I started small, working out of my garage, taking on freelance projects to fund my venture. The incubator provided the structure and support I needed to grow."

He added, "One of the biggest lessons I learned was the

importance of adaptability. The startup world is unpredictable, and being able to pivot and respond to market needs is crucial. Also, don't underestimate the power of networking. Building relationships with other entrepreneurs, mentors, and potential clients can open doors you never imagined."

Alex absorbed their stories, feeling a mix of inspiration and determination. The incubator offered workshops, mentorship programs, and access to potential investors, all of which Alex eagerly participated in. The journey of starting a business was challenging, but the community and resources provided a solid foundation.

One evening, after an intense brainstorming session with fellow entrepreneurs, Alex found themselves reflecting on their progress. The incubator had become a second home, a place where ideas flourished, and dreams took shape. They had learned to write a business plan, pitch to investors, and navigate the complexities of running a startup.

The support and camaraderie within the incubator were invaluable. Alex recalled a particularly tough day when they faced setbacks with their initial product prototype. Feeling disheartened, they sought advice from Kate.

"Setbacks are part of the journey, Alex," Kate had said, her tone reassuring. "Every successful entrepreneur has faced failures and obstacles. What matters is how you learn from them and keep pushing forward. Remember, building an empire takes time, resilience, and unwavering belief in your vision."

Tom had also offered words of wisdom. "Focus on your core strengths and don't hesitate to seek help when needed.

Surround yourself with a team that complements your skills and shares your passion. And always keep an eye on the market trends; staying relevant is key to sustained growth."

With renewed determination, Alex continued to refine their business idea. They spent countless hours researching, testing, and iterating, driven by the dream of creating something impactful. The incubator provided not just the technical knowledge but also the emotional support needed to navigate the highs and lows of entrepreneurship.

Months passed, and Alex's hard work began to pay off. They secured seed funding from an investor who believed in their vision, and their product started gaining traction. The initial challenges and sleepless nights were starting to feel worth it as their startup took its first steps toward becoming a successful venture.

Reflecting on their journey, Alex realized that building an empire wasn't just about financial success. It was about the courage to take risks, the willingness to learn and adapt, and the determination to pursue one's passion despite the challenges. The stories of Kate and Tom, along with the support from the incubator, had taught Alex the true essence of entrepreneurship.

As Alex stood in the bustling incubator, surrounded by fellow dreamers and doers, they felt a profound sense of belonging. The journey was far from over, but with each passing day, they were building their empire, one step at a time. And with the knowledge, resilience, and community they had gained, Alex was ready to take on whatever the future held.

Building Your Empire

1. **Ignition of Entrepreneurial Spark**:
   - Financial literacy workshops can inspire and ignite entrepreneurial aspirations.
   - Joining a startup incubator can provide a supportive environment to transform ideas into successful businesses.
2. **Value of Mentorship and Networking**:
   - Mentorship from experienced entrepreneurs like Kate and Tom is invaluable.
   - Networking with other entrepreneurs, mentors, and potential clients can open unexpected doors and opportunities.
3. **Starting Small and Growing**:
   - Successful entrepreneurs often start with small, manageable projects and gradually scale up.
   - Initial growth may be slow, but persistence and belief in the vision are crucial.
4. **Importance of Adaptability**:
   - The startup world is unpredictable, requiring entrepreneurs to pivot and respond to market needs.

- Flexibility and adaptability are essential for long-term success.

5. **Power of Community and Resources**:
   - Incubators provide essential resources such as workshops, mentorship programs, and access to potential investors.
   - The support and camaraderie within the incubator community help navigate challenges.

6. **Handling Setbacks and Failures**:
   - Setbacks and obstacles are part of the entrepreneurial journey.
   - Learning from failures and maintaining resilience are key to overcoming challenges.

7. **Focus on Core Strengths**:
   - Entrepreneurs should focus on their core strengths and seek help when needed.
   - Building a complementary team that shares the vision and passion is crucial.

8. **Staying Relevant and Informed**:
   - Keeping an eye on market trends and staying relevant is important for sustained growth.
   - Continuous research, testing, and iteration are necessary for product development.

10. **Securing Funding and Traction**:

- Hard work and perseverance can lead to securing seed funding and gaining traction.
- Convincing investors requires a clear vision and demonstrated potential.

11. **Essence of Entrepreneurship**:

- Building an empire is about more than financial success; it involves courage, learning, and determination.
- Pursuing one's passion despite challenges is a fundamental aspect of entrepreneurship.

12. **Belonging and Purpose**:

- Being part of a community of dreamers and doers provides a sense of belonging.
- The journey of building an empire is ongoing, driven by knowledge, resilience, and a supportive community.

Chapter 6

Unveiling the Tax Code

It was a rainy Saturday afternoon, and Alex found him self scrolling through a list of documentaries, looking for something both educational and engaging. After a week filled with work and business planning, he needed a change of pace. A title caught his eye: “Unveiling the Tax Code: The Evolution of Taxation and Its Impact on Societies.” Intrigued by the promise of historical insights, Alex settled in with a cup of tea and pressed on to play.

The documentary began with a sweeping overview of ancient civilizations, illustrating how taxation had been a fundamental aspect of society since the earliest recorded history. Mesopotamian tablets showed records of grain levies, while Egyptian hieroglyphs depicted tax collectors assessing crops along the Nile.

As the narrator’s voice filled the room, Alex became engrossed in the stories of ancient tax systems. The documentary explored how these early taxes funded essential public goods such as irrigation systems, defense, and religious temples. But it also highlighted the burden they placed on ordinary citizens, sometimes leading to social unrest and rebellion.

The scene shifted to ancient Rome, where Alex learned about the Roman Empire's sophisticated tax apparatus. Taxes in Rome were multifaceted, including customs duties, property taxes, and taxes on goods and services. The documentary explained how these revenues financed the empire's vast infrastructure, including roads, aqueducts, and public baths. However, the heavy tax burden on provinces sometimes sparked revolts, showcasing the delicate balance between taxation and public consent.

"Taxation has always been a double-edged sword," the narrator intoned. "It can build empires, but it can also bring them down."

As the documentary progressed, it delved into the medieval period, where feudal lords-imposed taxes on peasants, often in the form of labor or produce. Alex watched reenactments of tax collectors visiting villages, demanding tributes from struggling farmers. The inequities of the system were stark, emphasizing how taxation could exacerbate social divides.

The narrative moved forward to the Enlightenment era, where thinkers like Adam Smith began to articulate principles of fair taxation. Smith's ideas about the importance of equity, efficiency, and transparency in tax systems laid the groundwork for modern economic thought. Alex found this particularly fascinating, seeing how historical ideas continued to shape contemporary tax policies.

The documentary then turned to the American Revolution, highlighting how oppressive British taxes without representation fueled the colonies' desire for independence. Iconic events like the Boston Tea Party were dramatized, underscoring how taxation could ignite fundamental changes in governance and societal structure.

"Taxation isn't just about money," a historian commented. "It's about power, justice, and the relationship between the governed and those who govern."

Alex watched as the documentary transitioned to the Industrial Revolution, exploring how the rapid economic changes necessitated new tax policies. Progressive taxation emerged as a response to the growing wealth inequality, aiming to redistribute wealth more fairly across society. The narrator discussed how these policies evolved through trial and error, reflecting society's ongoing struggle to balance economic growth with social equity.

The modern era brought the story closer to Alex's own experience. The documentary covered the development of income taxes, corporate taxes, and sales taxes in the 20th century. It showed how governments used these revenues to fund social programs, infrastructure, and public services. However, it also touched on the complexities and controversies of contemporary tax policies, including tax evasion, loopholes, and the debate over tax rates.

Alex found the section on global taxation particularly enlightening. The documentary explained how different countries approached taxation, from the high taxes and extensive welfare programs in Scandinavian countries to the relatively low tax rates and limited social safety nets in others.

The comparisons illustrated how tax policies reflect broader societal values and priorities.

As the documentary concluded, it emphasized the ongoing evolution of tax systems. "Taxation will continue to change as societies evolve," the narrator stated. "Understanding its history helps us navigate its future."

The credits rolled, but Alex's mind was abuzz with new insights. The documentary had shed light on the profound impact of tax policies on economic dynamics and societal structures. It had illustrated how taxes could fund essential public services, promote social equity, and drive economic growth. But it had also highlighted the potential for misuse and the need for fair and transparent systems.

Alex realized that understanding taxation was crucial not just for personal finance but for comprehending broader economic and social issues. The lessons from history underscored the importance of informed and engaged citizens in shaping fair and effective tax policies.

Feeling inspired, Alex decided to delve deeper into the subject. They made a mental note to explore more resources on taxation, both historical and contemporary. The documentary had unveiled the tax code, revealing its complexities and its central role in shaping societies throughout the ages.

As the rain continued to patter against the window, Alex felt a sense of clarity and purpose. The journey to financial literacy had taken another significant step forward, one that would undoubtedly influence their personal and professional life. Understanding the power and implications of taxation was part of building their own empire, and Alex was eager to continue learning and growing.

Unveiling the Tax Code

1. **Historical Importance of Taxation**:
    - Taxation has been a fundamental aspect of society since ancient civilizations.
    - Early taxes funded essential public goods such as irrigation systems, defense, and religious temples.
2. **Double-Edged Sword of Taxation**:
    - Taxation can build empires by funding infrastructure and public services.
    - However, heavy tax burdens can lead to social unrest and rebellion.
3. **Tax Systems in Ancient Civilizations**:
    - Ancient Rome had a sophisticated tax apparatus, including customs duties, property taxes, and taxes on goods and services.
    - Medieval feudal lords imposed taxes on peasants, often exacerbating social divides.

5. **Principles of Fair Taxation**:

    - ➢ Enlightenment thinkers like Adam Smith laid the groundwork for modern tax policies with principles of equity, efficiency, and transparency.

    - ➢ Historical ideas continue to shape contemporary tax policies.

6. **Taxation and Governance**:

    - ➢ Oppressive taxes without representation fueled the American Revolution.

    - ➢ Taxation influences power, justice, and the relationship between the governed and those who govern.

7. **Economic Changes and Tax Policies**:

    - ➢ The Industrial Revolution necessitated new tax policies to address rapid economic changes and growing wealth inequality.

    - ➢ Progressive taxation emerged to redistribute wealth more fairly across society.

8. **Development of Modern Tax Systems**:

    - ➢ The 20th century saw the development of income taxes, corporate taxes, and sales taxes to fund social programs, infrastructure, and public services.

    - ➢ Contemporary tax policies are complex and often controversial, involving issues like tax evasion and loopholes.

9. **Global Taxation Approaches**:

   - Different countries have varying tax policies, reflecting broader societal values and priorities.

   - Comparisons of high-tax welfare states and low-tax countries highlight the impact of tax policies on social safety nets.

10. **Ongoing Evolution of Tax Systems**:

    - Tax systems continue to evolve as societies change.

    - Understanding the history of taxation helps navigate future tax policy developments.

11. **Impact on Economic and Social Issues**:

    - Tax policies profoundly impact economic dynamics and societal structures.

    - Taxes can fund essential public services, promote social equity, and drive economic growth.

12. **Need for Fair and Transparent Systems**:

    - Potential for misuse of tax systems highlights the need for fair and transparent tax policies.

    - Informed and engaged citizens play a crucial role in shaping effective tax policies.

14. **Personal and Professional Growth**:

- Understanding taxation is crucial for personal finance and broader economic and social issues.
- The journey to financial literacy includes comprehending the power and implications of taxation.

15. **Commitment to Continued Learning**:

- The documentary inspired a deeper exploration of taxation, both historical and contemporary.
- Ongoing education about tax systems is essential for building a secure financial future and contributing to informed public discourse.

Chapter 7

The Art of Wealth Creation

The room was filled with anticipation as Alex took a seat in the grand auditorium, eager for the seminar to begin. Titled "The Art of Wealth Creation," the seminar promised insights into how wealthy individuals generated income through various investment strategies. Alex had always been curious about the different avenues for wealth accumulation, and this seminar seemed like the perfect opportunity to learn from the experts.

As the lights dimmed, a charismatic speaker took the stage. He was introduced as Mr. Harrison, a seasoned investor and financial advisor with decades of experience. With a confident smile, Mr. Harrison greeted the audience and began his presentation.

"Welcome, everyone. Today, we're going to explore the fascinating world of wealth creation. Building wealth is not just about hard work; it's about smart work and creativity. The wealthy don't rely on a single income stream—they diversify. Let's dive into some of the key strategies."

He clicked a button on his remote, and a slide appeared on the screen, displaying the words: Real Estate.

"Real estate has long been a cornerstone of wealth building," Mr. Harrison explained. "Owning property can provide steady rental income and significant appreciation over time. But it's not just about buying and holding; there's an art to it."

He shared stories of individuals who had started with small investments in residential properties and gradually expanded to commercial real estate, leveraging their initial gains to scale up. He emphasized the importance of location, market research, and timing in real estate investments.

Alex took notes feverishly, fascinated by the stories of ordinary people who had built substantial wealth through strategic property investments. The idea of owning rental properties and earning passive income was particularly appealing.

The next slide featured the word: Stocks.

"Investing in stocks is another powerful way to build wealth," Mr. Harrison continued. "But it's not about gambling on hot tips. Successful investors do their homework. They analyze companies, understand market trends, and think long-term."

He explained different investment strategies, from dividend investing to growth stocks. He highlighted the importance of diversification, showing how a balanced portfolio could mitigate risks and enhance returns. Mr. Harrison also touched on the concept of compounding, illustrating how reinvesting dividends could significantly boost overall wealth over time.

Alex felt a sense of excitement. The stock market had always seemed intimidating, but Mr. Harrison's explanations made it more approachable. The idea of becoming a part-owner of successful companies and benefiting from their growth was compelling.

The seminar then shifted to a less conventional but equally intriguing topic: Intellectual Property.

"Intellectual property, or IP, is a unique and often overlooked avenue for wealth creation," Mr. Harrison said. "Patents, trademarks, copyrights, and royalties can generate substantial income streams."

He shared examples of inventors, authors, musicians, and entrepreneurs who had turned their ideas into profitable ventures. He discussed how patents could protect inventions and generate licensing fees, how trademarks could build brand value, and how copyrights could provide ongoing royalties from books, music, and other creative works.

Alex was particularly intrigued by the story of a young entrepreneur who had created a simple but innovative kitchen gadget. Through clever marketing and strategic licensing deals, the entrepreneur had turned a small invention into a multimillion-dollar business. The creativity and ingenuity involved in leveraging intellectual property opened Alex's eyes to new possibilities.

As the seminar continued, Mr. Harrison emphasized the importance of financial education and staying informed. "Wealth creation is an art, but it's also a science," he said. "The more you learn, the better equipped you'll be to make smart decisions. And remember, it's never too late to start."

He concluded the seminar by encouraging attendees to take action. "Identify your strengths, do your research, and start small. Diversify your investments and be patient. Wealth building is a journey, not a sprint."

The audience erupted into applause as Mr. Harrison left the stage. Alex felt a surge of motivation. The seminar had provided a wealth of knowledge and inspiration, showing that wealth creation was not reserved for the privileged few but was attainable through smart strategies and creative thinking.

On the way home, Alex reflected on the seminar. The stories of people transforming their lives through real estate, stocks, and intellectual property had broadened their understanding of wealth creation. It wasn't just about earning a paycheck; it was about making money work for you, exploring diverse opportunities, and thinking outside the box.

That evening, Alex began researching potential investments, from local real estate opportunities to promising stocks and intellectual property ideas. The seminar had ignited a new passion for financial growth and independence. Armed with the insights and inspiration from Mr. Harrison's seminar, Alex felt ready to embark on the artful journey of wealth creation, one strategic step at a time.

The Art of Wealth Creation

1. **Wealth Creation Through Diversification**:

    - Wealthy individuals generate income through multiple streams, not relying on a single source.
    - Diversification is essential to mitigate risks and enhance returns.

2. **Real Estate Investments**:

    - Real estate can provide steady rental income and significant appreciation over time.
    - Successful real estate investment requires strategic buying, holding, location analysis, market research, and timing.

3. **Investing in Stocks**:

    - Successful stock investment involves thorough analysis of companies, understanding market trends, and thinking long-term.
    - Different strategies include dividend investing and growth stocks.
    - Diversification within a stock portfolio can reduce risk.
    - Reinvesting dividends can significantly boost overall wealth through compounding.

4. **Leveraging Intellectual Property**:

   - Intellectual property (IP) such as patents, trademarks, copyrights, and royalties can be substantial income sources.
   - Protecting inventions with patents and generating licensing fees.
   - Building brand value with trademarks.
   - Earning ongoing royalties from creative works like books and music.

5. **Financial Education and Informed Decisions**:

   - Continuous financial education is crucial for making informed and smart decisions.
   - Staying informed and updated on financial trends and strategies helps in effective wealth creation.

6. **Starting Small and Scaling Up**:

   - Begin with small, manageable investments and gradually scale up as you gain experience and returns.
   - Identify personal strengths and areas of interest to guide investment choices.

7. **The Importance of Creativity and Ingenuity**:

   - Wealth creation involves creative thinking and innovative strategies.

- Exploring diverse opportunities and thinking outside the box can open new avenues for income.

8. **Patience and Long-Term Perspective**:

   - Building wealth is a journey that requires patience and a long-term perspective.

   - Consistent effort and strategic planning are essential for sustained financial growth.

9. **Taking Action and Being Proactive**:

   - Identifying strengths, conducting research, and taking informed actions are key steps in wealth creation.

   - Proactive financial management and seizing opportunities contribute to financial independence.

10. **Empowerment Through Knowledge**:

    - Financial education empowers individuals to take control of their financial future.

    - Knowledge and strategic action make wealth creation accessible and attainable for everyone.

11. **Ongoing Motivation and Passion**:

    - The seminar ignited a new passion in Alex for financial growth and independence.

- Continued learning and exploration of potential investments drives ongoing motivation for wealth creation.

Chapter 8

Knowledge as Currency

The sun was just beginning to rise as Alex arrived at the sleek downtown office of Sterling Financial Services. Today marked the start of a new chapter in Alex's journey toward financial mastery. After months of studying and attending seminars, Alex had secured an apprenticeship with Mr. Collins, a highly respected financial advisor known for his expertise and dedication to continuous learning.

Mr. Collins welcomed Alex with a firm handshake and a warm smile. "Welcome, Alex. I'm glad you're here. Our work together will be demanding but incredibly rewarding. Are you ready to dive in?"

"Absolutely," Alex replied, eager to absorb as much knowledge as possible.

The first week was a whirlwind of activity. Alex shadowed Mr. Collins in client meetings, attended team strategy sessions, and pored over financial reports. Each day presented a new learning opportunity, and Alex quickly realized that the world of finance was far more intricate and dynamic than they had imagined.

One afternoon, after a particularly intense meeting, Mr. Collins invited Alex into his office for a debriefing. "Alex, do you know what sets successful financial advisors apart from the rest?" he asked, leaning back in his chair.

Alex thought for a moment. "Experience? Client relationships?"

"Those are important," Mr. Collins agreed, "but the real key is continuous learning and adaptability. The financial world is constantly evolving. New regulations, market shifts, technological advancements—if you're not learning, you're falling behind."

He reached for a book on his desk and handed it to Alex. "This is one of my favorites on investment strategies. Read it, and we'll discuss it next week."

Alex accepted the book, feeling both excited and a little daunted. Over the following days, Alex dove into the pages, absorbing concepts and strategies that were new and challenging. True to his word, Mr. Collins discussed the book with Alex, providing deeper insights and relating the theories to real-world applications.

Weeks turned into months, and Alex's understanding of finance grew exponentially. Mr. Collins introduced Alex to a wide range of topics, from portfolio management and risk assessment to estate planning and tax strategies. Each lesson was grounded in real-life scenarios, illustrating the practical implications of financial theories.

One day, during a quiet moment between meetings, Alex asked, "Mr. Collins, how do you stay so up to date with everything? It seems like there's always something new to learn."

Mr. Collins smiled. "That's because there is always something new to learn. I read extensively, attend conferences, and network with other professionals. But more than that, I approach each day with a mindset of curiosity and openness. The moment you think you know everything, you stop growing."

He paused, then added, "Knowledge is like currency. The more you have, the more valuable you become. But unlike money, knowledge can be shared without diminishing your own wealth. In fact, sharing what you know can lead to even greater insights and opportunities."

Inspired by this philosophy, Alex embraced the habit of continuous learning. They began attending evening classes, subscribing to financial journals, and joining professional groups. The more Alex learned, the more they realized how much there was still to discover.

One particularly transformative experience came when Mr. Collins took Alex to a financial conference in New York City. The event was a gathering of some of the brightest minds in the industry, featuring panel discussions, workshops, and networking sessions. Alex listened intently to the speakers, absorbing their wisdom and innovative ideas.

During a break, Mr. Collins introduced Alex to several of his colleagues. "This is Alex, my apprentice. They've got a real passion for learning and a sharp mind for finance."

One of the seasoned advisors smiled and said, "The best advice I can give you, Alex, is to never stop asking questions. The market rewards those who are not only knowledgeable but also adaptable. The financial landscape is always shifting, and your ability to navigate those changes will define your success."

That night, back at the hotel, Alex reflected on the day's events. The conference reinforced the importance of expertise and adaptability. It was clear that the path to sustained financial success was paved with continuous learning and the ability to adjust to new circumstances.

As the apprenticeship progressed, Alex grew more confident in their abilities. They started taking on more responsibilities, from advising clients under Mr. Collins's supervision to developing investment strategies. With each new task, Alex applied the principles of continuous learning and adaptability, always seeking to expand their knowledge and improve their skills.

By the end of the apprenticeship, Alex had not only gained a wealth of financial knowledge but also developed a mindset that valued education and flexibility. Mr. Collins's mentorship had been instrumental in shaping this perspective, demonstrating that knowledge truly was a form of currency—one that could unlock endless possibilities and drive sustained success.

On the final day of the apprenticeship, Mr. Collins gave Alex a parting gift: a leather-bound journal. "Use this to document your journey," he said. "Write down what you learn, reflect on your experiences, and set goals for the future. Your career is just beginning, and I have no doubt you'll achieve great things."

Alex thanked Mr. Collins, feeling a deep sense of gratitude and readiness. Armed with the lessons of continuous learning and adaptability, they were prepared to face the future with confidence. The journey ahead was sure to be challenging, but with knowledge as their currency, Alex felt equipped to build a prosperous and fulfilling career.

Knowledge as Currency

1. **Continuous Learning and Adaptability**:
   - The financial world is constantly evolving, requiring ongoing education and adaptability.
   - Successful financial advisors prioritize continuous learning to stay current with new regulations, market shifts, and technological advancements.
2. **Value of Knowledge**:
   - Knowledge is like currency; the more you have, the more valuable you become.
   - Unlike money, sharing knowledge can lead to even greater insights and opportunities.

4. **Practical Application of Theories**:

   ➢ Understanding financial theories is important, but applying them in real-world scenarios is crucial.

   ➢ Engaging with practical examples helps deepen understanding and improve skills.

5. **Mindset of Curiosity and Openness**:

   ➢ Approach each day with a mindset of curiosity and openness.

   ➢ Acknowledge that there is always something new to learn, which prevents stagnation and promotes growth.

6. **Importance of Asking Questions**:

   ➢ Continuously asking questions and seeking answers is vital in navigating the ever-changing financial landscape.

   ➢ Being knowledgeable and adaptable are key components to success in finance.

7. **Networking and Professional Development**:

   ➢ Attending conferences, networking with professionals, and joining professional groups enhance knowledge and provide new perspectives.

   ➢ Engaging with industry peers helps in staying informed about the latest trends and innovations.

9. **Comprehensive Financial Knowledge**:

    - Gaining a broad understanding of various financial topics, such as portfolio management, risk assessment, estate planning, and tax strategies, is essential.
    - A well-rounded knowledge base allows for better decision-making and client advising.

10. **Mentorship and Guidance**:

    - Having a mentor like Mr. Collins provides invaluable guidance and accelerates learning.
    - Mentorship helps in developing a strategic approach to learning and applying financial concepts.

11. **Documenting and Reflecting on Learning**:

    - Keeping a journal to document learning, reflect on experiences, and set future goals is beneficial for continuous improvement.
    - Reflection helps in consolidating knowledge and identifying areas for further growth.

12. **Building Confidence and Taking on Responsibilities**:

    - Gaining knowledge and skills through continuous learning builds confidence.
    - Taking on more responsibilities, such as advising clients and developing investment strategies, reinforces learning and enhances expertise.

13. **Long-Term Success Through Education and Flexibility**:

   - A mindset that values education and flexibility is crucial for sustained financial success.

   - Continuous learning and adaptability are key to navigating future challenges and opportunities in the financial industry.

14. **Preparedness for the Future**:

   - With knowledge as their currency, individuals are better equipped to build a prosperous and fulfilling career.

   - The journey ahead may be challenging, but continuous learning and adaptability provide a strong foundation for success.

Chapter 9

Overcoming Challenges

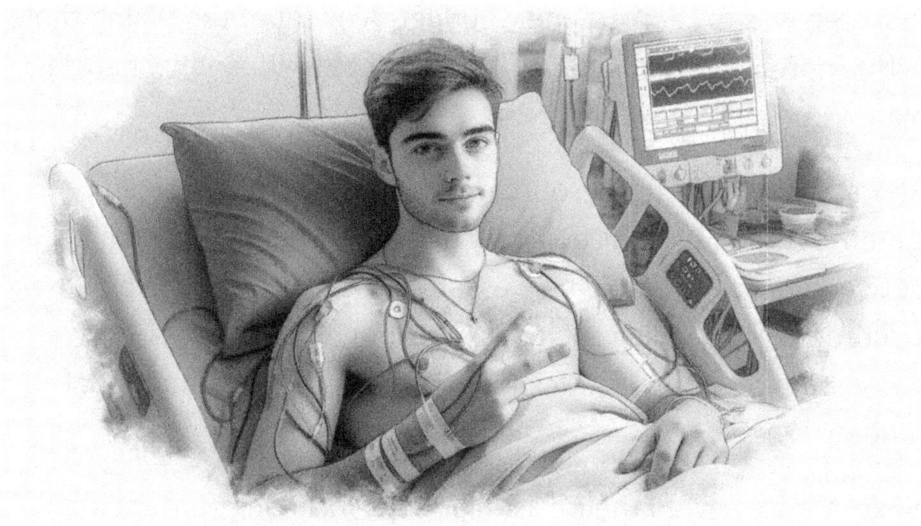

It was a typical Friday afternoon when Alex's phone buzzed with an incoming call from their doctor's office. The cheerful tone of the receptionist quickly turned somber as she explained the results of a recent check-up. "Alex, the tests indicate you need to undergo a minor surgery as soon as possible. It's nothing major, but it needs to be done."

Alex's heart sank. While the news was a relief in terms of health, the looming medical bills were a daunting prospect. As a young professional still building their financial foundation, this unexpected expense threatened to derail their carefully laid plans.

Over the weekend, Alex pored over the details of the medical bills, insurance coverage, and out-of-pocket costs. The total amount was staggering. Despite having some savings, it became clear that this setback would significantly impact their finances.

Determined to handle the situation with resilience, Alex turned to the lessons learned during the apprenticeship with Mr. Collins and the various financial resources they had encountered. The first step was to reassess their budget. Alex sat at the dining table with a notebook, pen, and laptop, ready to craft a new financial plan.

Alex started by listing all sources of income and categorizing expenses. They scrutinized every expenditure, distinguishing between necessities and non-essentials. By cutting back on discretionary spending such as dining out, subscriptions, and non-essential shopping, Alex found ways to free up additional funds.

Next, Alex reviewed their existing debts, including student loans and credit card balances. The priority was to avoid accumulating more debt due to the medical bills. Alex reached out to the hospital's billing department to discuss a payment plan. Negotiating lower monthly payments provided some breathing room while ensuring the debt was managed responsibly.

Realizing the importance of an emergency fund, Alex decided to set aside a portion of their income specifically for unforeseen expenses. Despite the immediate financial strain, Alex committed to regularly contributing even a small amount to this fund. This habit would help buffer future financial shocks.

Remembering the value of expert guidance, Alex scheduled a meeting with a financial planner recommended by Mr. Collins. During the session, the planner helped Alex develop a comprehensive strategy to tackle the current financial challenge while setting long-term goals. They discussed the benefits of diversifying income streams, the potential for side gigs, and the importance of continuous financial education.

Alex dove into financial planning resources, devouring books, articles, and online courses. One particularly helpful book on personal finance offered practical advice on managing medical debt, emphasizing communication with creditors and exploring financial assistance programs. Alex learned about negotiating medical bills and seeking out charitable organizations that could provide support.

The journey was far from easy. There were moments of stress and frustration as Alex juggled medical appointments, work responsibilities, and financial planning. However, maintaining a positive mindset and focusing on incremental progress helped Alex stay resilient. Regular check-ins with the financial planner provided motivation and reassurance.

Months passed, and Alex's diligence began to pay off. The medical debt was gradually being reduced through consistent payments. The revised budget allowed Alex to maintain a semblance of normalcy without sacrificing essential needs. Meanwhile, the budding emergency fund provided a sense of security and peace of mind.

The experience taught Alex invaluable lessons about resilience and financial management. Unexpected setbacks were a part of life, but with careful planning, resourcefulness, and a proactive approach, they could be navigated successfully. Alex emerged from the ordeal with a deeper understanding of personal finance and a strengthened resolve to achieve financial stability.

One evening, as Alex reviewed the now-stable financial plan, a sense of accomplishment washed over them. The initial panic had transformed into a structured approach, proving that challenges could be overcome with knowledge and determination.

Reflecting on the journey, Alex felt a renewed sense of purpose. The skills and strategies acquired during this challenging time were not just temporary solutions but lifelong tools. Alex knew that future challenges would inevitably arise, but with the foundation of financial literacy and resilience, they were well-equipped to face whatever came their way.

As the sun set on another day, Alex closed the notebook with a sense of fulfillment. The chapter of overcoming financial setbacks was not just a story of survival but a testament to the power of resilience and the importance of continuous learning. With a clear plan and a resilient spirit, Alex was ready to continue building a secure and prosperous future.

Overcoming Challenges

1. **Resilience in the Face of Unexpected Expenses**:
    - Financial setbacks, such as unexpected medical bills, require resilience and proactive planning.
    - Maintaining a positive mindset and focusing on incremental progress is crucial.

3. **Reevaluating the Budget**:

   - List all sources of income and categorize expenses.
   - Distinguish between necessities and non-essentials, cutting back on discretionary spending to free up additional funds.

4. **Managing Debt**:

   - Review existing debts and avoid accumulating more debt due to unexpected expenses.
   - Negotiate with creditors or service providers to establish manageable payment plans.

5. **Building an Emergency Fund**:

   - Regularly contribute to an emergency fund, even in small amounts, to buffer future financial shocks.
   - An emergency fund provides security and peace of mind during unforeseen financial challenges.

6. **Seeking Financial Advice**:

   - Consult with financial planners to develop comprehensive strategies for managing financial challenges and setting long-term goals.
   - Diversifying income streams and considering side gigs can provide additional financial stability.

8. **Utilizing Financial Planning Resources**:

   - Explore financial planning books, articles, and online courses to gain practical advice and strategies.

   - Learn about managing medical debt, negotiating bills, and seeking financial assistance from charitable organizations.

9. **Maintaining Resilience and Determination**:

   - Stay resilient by maintaining a structured approach to financial management.

   - Regular check-ins with financial advisors provide motivation and reassurance.

10. **Structured Financial Planning**:

    - Transform initial panic into a structured approach for managing financial setbacks.

    - Consistent payments and a revised budget help in reducing debt and maintaining financial normalcy.

11. **Lifelong Financial Tools**:

    - Skills and strategies acquired during financial challenges become lifelong tools for managing future setbacks.

    - Financial literacy and resilience provide a strong foundation for long-term financial stability.

13. **Proactive Approach and Resourcefulness**:

- Addressing financial challenges with a proactive approach and resourcefulness leads to successful navigation of setbacks.
- A sense of accomplishment and fulfillment comes from overcoming challenges through knowledge and determination.

14. **Continuous Learning and Adaptability**:

- Continuous learning and adaptability are key to managing unexpected financial challenges.
- Regularly updating financial knowledge and strategies helps in facing future uncertainties.

15. **Sense of Purpose and Fulfillment**:

- Overcoming financial setbacks reinforces a sense of purpose and commitment to building a secure future.
- A clear financial plan and resilient spirit are essential for continued financial growth and stability.

Chapter 10

Setting Sail on Your Financial Journey

The sun was just rising as Alex sat at their kitchen table, sipping a cup of freshly brewed coffee. Today was a significant day. After months of learning, navigating financial challenges, and gathering wisdom from mentors, Alex was ready to create a personalized financial plan. It was time to set sail on their financial journey with a clear course charted ahead.

With a deep breath, Alex opened their laptop and began organizing the notes and resources they had accumulated. The first step was to define clear, achievable financial goals. Alex had learned from Mr. Collins and various financial planning resources that setting specific goals was crucial for creating a roadmap to financial success.

1. Setting Financial Goals

Alex decided to categorize their goals into short-term, medium-term, and long-term objectives:

Short-Term Goals (1-2 years):

- Build an emergency fund equivalent to six months of living expenses.
- Pay off the remaining medical bills and credit card debt.
- Save for a professional certification course to enhance career prospects.

Medium-Term Goals (3-5 years):

- Save for a down payment on a home.
- Establish a diversified investment portfolio.
- Start a side business to generate additional income.

Long-Term Goals (10+ years):

- Save for retirement, aiming to contribute the maximum amount to a retirement account each year.
- Fund future travel and educational opportunities.
- Ensure financial security for future family needs, including children's education.

2. Starting an Investment Portfolio

With goals in place, Alex turned to the next significant step: starting an investment portfolio. Recalling the investment seminar and the advice from Mr. Harrison, Alex understood the importance of diversification and a long-term perspective.

Step-by-Step Investment Plan:

- Research and Education: Alex committed to continuing

their education on investment strategies. They subscribed to financial news, joined online forums, and took online courses on stock market basics, real estate investing, and portfolio management.

- Choosing a Brokerage Account: Alex selected a reputable online brokerage that offered low fees, a user-friendly interface, and educational resources.
- Initial Investments: With the help of a financial planner, Alex decided to start with a mix of low-cost index funds and ETFs, which provided broad market exposure and minimized risk. They allocated a small portion to individual stocks in sectors they were interested in, like technology and renewable energy.
- Automated Contributions: Alex set up automated monthly contributions to their investment account, ensuring consistent growth of the portfolio over time.

3. Establishing a Savings Strategy

Next, Alex focused on establishing a robust savings strategy. They knew from their experiences and guidance from mentors that a disciplined approach to saving was essential for achieving financial goals.

Savings Strategy Components:

- Emergency Fund: Alex prioritized building an emergency fund. They opened a high-yield savings account specifically for this purpose, setting up automatic transfers from their checking account each month until they reached their goal of six months of living expenses.

- High-Interest Debt: To tackle their remaining medical bills and credit card debt, Alex used the debt avalanche method, focusing on paying off the highest-interest debt first while making minimum payments on the rest. This strategy helped reduce overall interest costs and accelerate debt repayment.
- Goal-Specific Savings: For medium-term goals like the down payment on a home, Alex opened separate savings accounts. They created a budget that allocated a portion of their monthly income to these accounts, ensuring steady progress towards each goal.
- Retirement Savings: Alex set up automatic contributions to a retirement account, taking full advantage of employer matching programs and aiming to increase their contributions annually.

4. Leveraging Online Resources and Mentorship

Throughout this process, Alex leveraged a wealth of online resources and mentorship. They regularly consulted with Mr. Collins and other financial advisors, attended webinars, and participated in online communities focused on personal finance and investing.

Mentorship and Resources:

- Financial Mentors: Regular check-ins with Mr. Collins provided valuable feedback and guidance. His advice on staying adaptable and informed proved invaluable as Alex navigated their financial plan.
- Online Communities: Engaging with online forums and

groups allowed Alex to learn from the experiences of others, ask questions, and share their progress.

- Educational Platforms: Websites offering free courses, articles, and tools for financial planning became Alex's go-to resources for continuous learning.

5. Staying the Course and Adapting

As Alex reviewed their personalized financial plan, they felt a sense of accomplishment and clarity. However, they knew that the journey had just begun. The financial plan was not a static document but a dynamic guide that would evolve with their life circumstances and goals.

Staying the Course:

- Regular Reviews: Alex scheduled quarterly reviews of their financial plan, adjusting their strategies and goals as needed based on changes in income, expenses, and market conditions.
- Continuous Learning: They committed to ongoing education, staying informed about new financial products, investment opportunities, and economic trends.
- Flexibility: Alex understood the importance of being flexible and adapting to unexpected challenges. The resilience they had built from overcoming medical bills would serve them well in future financial decisions.
- As the sun set, Alex closed the laptop, feeling a profound sense of readiness. With a clear plan, a commitment to continuous learning, and the support of mentors and

resources, Alex was set to sail on their financial journey. The path ahead was sure to have its challenges, but armed with knowledge and a well-crafted plan, Alex was confident in their ability to navigate the waters and achieve financial success.

Setting Sail on Your Financial Journey

1. **Setting Financial Goals**:

   - Categorizing goals into short-term, medium-term, and long-term helps create a clear roadmap.

   - **Short-Term Goals**: Building an emergency fund, paying off medical bills and credit card debt, saving for professional certification.

   - **Medium-Term Goals**: Saving for a home down payment, establishing a diversified investment portfolio, starting a side business.

   - **Long-Term Goals**: Saving for retirement, funding future travel and education, ensuring financial security for future family needs.

2. **Starting an Investment Portfolio**:

   - **Research and Education**: Continuous learning about investment strategies, market basics, and portfolio management.
   - **Choosing a Brokerage**: Selecting a reputable

brokerage with low fees, user-friendly interface, and educational resources.

- **Initial Investments**: Starting with low-cost index funds and ETFs for broad market exposure and minimizing risk; allocating a small portion to individual stocks.
- **Automated Contributions**: Setting up automated monthly contributions to ensure consistent portfolio growth.

3. **Establishing a Savings Strategy**:

- **Emergency Fund**: Prioritizing an emergency fund in a high-yield savings account with automatic transfers.
- **High-Interest Debt**: Using the debt avalanche method to pay off high-interest debt first.
- **Goal-Specific Savings**: Opening separate savings accounts for medium-term goals and budgeting monthly income allocations.
- **Retirement Savings**: Setting up automatic retirement account contributions and maximizing employer matching programs.

4. **Leveraging Online Resources and Mentorship**:

- **Financial Mentors**: Regular check-ins with mentors like Mr. Collins for feedback and guidance.
- **Online Communities**: Engaging with online forums and groups for learning from others' experiences and sharing progress.

- **Educational Platforms**: Utilizing free courses, articles, and financial planning tools for continuous learning.

5. **Staying the Course and Adapting**:

    - **Regular Reviews**: Scheduling quarterly reviews of the financial plan to adjust strategies and goals based on changes in circumstances.
    - **Continuous Learning**: Committing to ongoing education about financial products, investment opportunities, and economic trends.
    - **Flexibility**: Being adaptable and resilient in the face of unexpected challenges, leveraging past experiences to inform future decisions.

Chapter 11

Seeking Advanced Horizons

Alex's financial journey had already taken them through the basics of budgeting, debt management, and starting an investment portfolio. With a solid foundation in place, Alex felt ready to explore more advanced financial concepts to maximize their wealth growth. The next step was to dive deeper into areas like tax-efficient investing, asset allocation strategies, and risk management techniques. Armed with a thirst for knowledge, Alex embarked on this new phase with enthusiasm.

1. Tax-Efficient Investing

One of the first concepts Alex delved into was tax-efficient investing. Understanding that taxes could significantly impact investment returns, Alex sought to learn how to optimize their portfolio for tax savings.

Online Courses and Research:

- **Tax-Advantaged Accounts:** Alex enrolled in an online course that covered various tax-advantaged accounts such as IRAs, Roth IRAs, and 401(k)s. They learned about the benefits of these accounts, including tax-deferred growth and tax-free withdrawals in retirement. Alex decided to maximize contributions to these accounts to take full advantage of the tax benefits.

- **Tax-Loss Harvesting:** Another course introduced Alex to the concept of tax-loss harvesting, a strategy to offset capital gains with capital losses. By strategically selling underperforming investments, Alex could reduce their taxable income and reinvest the proceeds into similar assets.

- **Qualified Dividends and Long-Term Capital Gains:** Alex learned the importance of holding investments for more than a year to benefit from the lower tax rates on qualified dividends and long-term capital gains. This knowledge influenced their investment decisions, encouraging a long-term approach.

2. Asset Allocation Strategies

Next, Alex focused on asset allocation strategies to optimize their investment portfolio. They understood that diversification was crucial to managing risk and maximizing returns.

Seminars and Workshops:

- **Modern Portfolio Theory (MPT):** Attending a financial seminar, Alex was introduced to Modern Portfolio Theory, which emphasizes the importance of diversifying investments across different asset classes to achieve the highest possible return for a given level of risk. The seminar covered concepts like the efficient frontier, risk-return tradeoff, and correlation between assets.

- **Strategic vs. Tactical Asset Allocation:** Another workshop highlighted the difference between strategic and tactical asset allocation. Strategic asset allocation involves setting long-term investment goals and maintaining a consistent asset mix, while tactical asset allocation allows for short-term adjustments based on market conditions. Alex decided to adopt a strategic approach with periodic reviews to make tactical adjustments as needed.
- **Global Diversification:** Alex also learned about the benefits of global diversification. Investing in international markets could reduce the risk associated with economic downturns in any single country. They began researching international mutual funds and ETFs to include in their portfolio.

3. Risk Management Techniques

To further safeguard their growing wealth, Alex explored advanced risk management techniques. Managing risk effectively was essential to preserving capital and ensuring long-term financial stability.

Advanced Financial Courses:

- **Hedging Strategies:** An online course on derivatives introduced Alex to hedging strategies using options and futures. While these instruments were more complex, Alex appreciated their potential to protect against downside risk. They decided to use options conservatively, primarily for hedging rather than speculative purposes.

- **Insurance Planning:** Another important aspect of risk management was insurance planning. Alex attended a seminar on comprehensive insurance coverage, including health, life, disability, and property insurance. Understanding the importance of protecting their assets and income, Alex reviewed and updated their insurance policies to ensure adequate coverage.
- **Emergency Fund Enhancement:** Building on the emergency fund they had already established, Alex learned about creating a tiered emergency fund. This approach involved having a cash reserve for immediate needs and a more liquid investment fund for longer-term emergencies. This strategy provided both liquidity and growth potential.

4. Integrating Advanced Concepts

With a wealth of new knowledge, Alex set out to integrate these advanced concepts into their financial plan. They reviewed their current portfolio and made adjustments based on the principles of tax efficiency, asset allocation, and risk management.

Action Plan:

- **Maximizing Tax Efficiency:** Alex increased contributions to tax-advantaged accounts and implemented tax-loss harvesting where applicable. They also focused on holding investments long-term to benefit from favorable tax rates.
- **Diversified Asset Allocation:** Alex rebalanced their portfolio to achieve a diversified mix of domestic and

international stocks, bonds, and alternative investments. They set up a system for periodic reviews to make necessary adjustments.

Enhanced Risk Management: Alex added hedging strategies to their portfolio and ensured comprehensive insurance coverage. They also expanded their emergency fund to include a tiered approach, providing both immediate access to cash and longer-term security.

5. Continuous Learning and Adaptation

As Alex implemented these advanced strategies, they remained committed to continuous learning and adaptation. They regularly attended financial seminars, subscribed to industry publications, and participated in online forums to stay informed about the latest trends and developments.

Mentorship and Networking:

- **Seeking Guidance:** Alex continued to seek guidance from Mr. Collins and other mentors, valuing their insights and experience. Regular check-ins provided valuable feedback and helped Alex stay on track.
- **Networking with Peers:** Engaging with other financial enthusiasts and professionals allowed Alex to exchange ideas and learn from diverse perspectives. These interactions often led to new opportunities and strategies for wealth growth.

Exploring advanced financial concepts had been an enriching experience for Alex. The journey from basic financial literacy to mastering complex strategies had transformed their approach to wealth management. By embracing tax-efficient investing, strategic asset allocation, and sophisticated risk management techniques, Alex was well-equipped to maximize wealth growth and achieve long-term financial success.

As Alex set sail on this new phase of their financial journey, they felt confident and empowered. The knowledge gained and the strategies implemented would serve as a strong foundation for navigating the ever-evolving financial landscape. With a commitment to continuous learning and adaptability, Alex was ready to seize new opportunities and overcome future challenges, steering their financial ship toward a prosperous and secure future.

Chapter 12

Continuing the Adventure

The cool breeze of a late autumn afternoon swept through the park as Alex strolled along the path, deep in thought. The journey from a recent college graduate struggling with financial uncertainty to a confident investor and financial planner had been transformative. Reflecting on this personal growth, Alex felt a sense of fulfillment and purpose. But this adventure was far from over.

One evening, Alex decided to host a small gathering at their apartment. Inviting close friends and colleagues, Alex wanted to share the financial insights and strategies that had proven so valuable. As everyone settled into the cozy living room, Alex began to speak.

"Thank you all for coming. I wanted to share some of the financial lessons I've learned over the past few years. Managing money can seem daunting, but with the right knowledge and tools, it becomes much more manageable—and even exciting."

Alex started with the basics of budgeting and debt management, recounting personal experiences of overcoming financial setbacks and emphasizing the importance of an emergency fund. The conversation then moved to more advanced topics like tax-efficient investing and asset allocation strategies.

"What's crucial," Alex said, "is to never stop learning. The financial world is always changing, and staying informed is key to making smart decisions."

As the evening progressed, Alex encouraged their friends to embrace lifelong learning in financial management. They shared resources such as favorite books, online courses, and financial planning tools that had been instrumental in their journey.

"Knowledge is a powerful tool," Alex emphasized. "The more you learn, the more empowered you become to take control of your financial future. And remember, it's okay to seek help from professionals and mentors. Their guidance can make a huge difference."

Inspired by Alex's journey and insights, the group engaged in a lively discussion about their own financial goals and challenges. Alex realized that fostering a community of support and shared learning was incredibly rewarding.

Driven by the desire to continue learning and sharing knowledge, Alex sought out a community of like-minded individuals dedicated to ongoing financial education. They found a local financial literacy group that met regularly to discuss various aspects of personal finance, from budgeting basics to advanced investment strategies.

At the first meeting, Alex was welcomed by a diverse group of people, each with their own unique experiences and expertise. The atmosphere was collaborative and supportive, with everyone eager to learn from one another.

During the session, Alex shared their journey and the strategies that had helped them achieve financial stability. In turn, they listened to others' stories, gaining new perspectives and ideas.

"Continuing our financial education is a journey, not a destination," said the group's facilitator. "We're here to support each other, share insights, and grow together."

As Alex became more involved in the community, they forged strong connections with fellow members. These relationships provided a valuable support network, offering encouragement, advice, and accountability.

Alex also started mentoring newcomers to the group, sharing the lessons and strategies that had worked for them. This role not only reinforced their own knowledge but also gave Alex a sense of purpose and fulfillment.

One of the group's initiatives was to organize financial workshops for the wider community. Alex took an active role in planning and leading these workshops, covering topics like budgeting, investing, and retirement planning. Seeing the positive impact on participants reinforced Alex's commitment to financial education.

One quiet evening, Alex sat down to reflect on the incredible journey they had undertaken. From the uncertainty and challenges of early adulthood to the confidence and knowledge they now possessed, the transformation was profound.

Alex realized that the adventure of financial growth and education was ongoing. Each new piece of knowledge opened doors to further learning and opportunities. The sense of community and the joy of helping others achieve their financial goals added a new dimension to Alex's journey.

As Alex looked to the future, they felt excited about the endless possibilities. They planned to continue their own education, exploring new areas of finance and staying abreast of industry trends. Alex also aimed to expand their mentoring efforts, helping more people navigate their financial journeys.

Joining professional organizations and attending conferences were also on Alex's agenda. These activities would provide fresh insights, foster new connections, and keep the spirit of lifelong learning alive.

Alex's financial journey was a testament to the power of knowledge, resilience, and community. Reflecting on their growth, Alex felt a profound sense of gratitude for the mentors, resources, and experiences that had shaped their path.

But most importantly, Alex understood that the adventure was far from over. With each step, they were not only building their own financial future but also inspiring and empowering others to do the same. The commitment to lifelong learning and community support would continue to guide Alex as they navigated the ever-evolving landscape of personal finance.

As Alex set out on this continuing adventure, they felt ready to embrace the challenges and opportunities ahead, confident in their ability to achieve financial success and help others along the way.

Continuing the Adventure

1. **Transformative Personal Growth**:
    - Transition from financial uncertainty to confidence and financial planning.
    - Reflection on personal growth brings fulfillment and purpose.
2. **Sharing Knowledge**:
    - Hosting gatherings to share financial insights and strategies is valuable.
    - Discussing budgeting, debt management, emergency funds, tax-efficient investing, and asset allocation with peers fosters collective growth.
3. **Lifelong Learning**:
    - Embrace lifelong learning in financial management.
    - The financial world is always changing; staying informed is key to making smart decisions.

- Seek out resources like books, online courses, and financial planning tools.

4. Empowerment Through Knowledge:
   - Knowledge empowers individuals to take control of their financial future.
   - Seeking help from professionals and mentors is beneficial.

5. Community Support:
   - Fostering a community of support and shared learning is rewarding.
   - Joining a financial literacy group provides a collaborative and supportive environment for learning.

6. Mentorship:
   - Mentoring newcomers reinforces one's own knowledge and provides a sense of purpose and fulfillment.
   - Sharing lessons and strategies helps others achieve financial stability.

7. Organizing Workshops:
   - Organizing and leading financial workshops for the community reinforces commitment to financial education.

- Topics covered include budgeting, investing, and retirement planning.

8. **Reflecting on the Journey**:

   - Reflecting on the journey from early adulthood challenges to current confidence and knowledge highlights personal transformation.

   - Each piece of knowledge opens doors to further learning and opportunities.

9. **Ongoing Adventure**:

   - The adventure of financial growth and education is ongoing.

   - Planning to continue education, explore new areas of finance, and stay abreast of industry trends is essential.

10. **Expanding Mentoring Efforts**:

    - Helping more people navigate their financial journeys enhances the sense of community and shared growth.

    - Joining professional organizations and attending conferences provide fresh insights and new connections.

11. **Gratitude and Commitment**:

    - Reflecting on growth brings a sense of gratitude for mentors, resources, and experiences.

- The commitment to lifelong learning and community support guides the continued financial journey.

12. **Inspiring and Empowering Others**:

    - Building one's financial future while inspiring and empowering others is fulfilling.
    - The ongoing commitment to education and community support is crucial for navigating personal finance.

13. **Embracing Challenges and Opportunities**:

    - Embracing future challenges and opportunities with confidence is key.
    - The journey continues with a focus on achieving financial success and helping others along the way.

Chapter 13

The Journey's End

The morning sun cast a warm glow over the tranquil park where Alex sat on a bench, reflecting on the remarkable journey that had brought them here. The park had always been a place of solace and contemplation, and today it felt particularly fitting as Alex pondered the transformation from financial uncertainty to confidence and independence.

Alex's journey had been marked by significant milestones, each representing a step closer to financial stability and independence. One of the most memorable milestones was the day Alex made the final payment on their student loans. They remembered the weight that lifted off their shoulders, symbolizing the end of a long chapter of financial obligation and the beginning of true financial freedom.

"I did it," Alex whispered to themselves, a smile spreading across their face. The achievement was a testament to their perseverance and disciplined financial planning.

Another major milestone was the completion of their emergency fund, which now held six months' worth of living expenses. This fund had been a cornerstone of Alex's financial strategy, providing a safety net that allowed them to take calculated risks and seize new opportunities.

Achieving financial independence had always been Alex's ultimate goal. Through careful budgeting, strategic investments, and continuous learning, Alex had built a diversified portfolio that generated enough passive income to cover their living expenses. This financial independence meant that Alex could now focus on passions and pursuits without the constant pressure of financial instability.

Reflecting on the years of diligent saving and investing, Alex felt a deep sense of accomplishment. The journey had been challenging, with moments of doubt and setbacks, but each challenge had taught valuable lessons and strengthened Alex's resolve.

With a solid foundation and a wealth of knowledge, Alex felt a growing desire to give back to the community that had supported them. Remembering the impact mentors like Mr. Collins and Ms. Martinez had on their own journey, Alex resolved to mentor others and promote financial literacy in their community.

Alex began by volunteering at local schools, offering workshops on budgeting, saving, and investing. The sessions were interactive and engaging, filled with real-life examples and practical tips. Alex found immense satisfaction in seeing the spark of understanding in students' eyes and knowing they were helping to lay the groundwork for their future financial success.

In addition to working with students, Alex also started a financial literacy blog, sharing insights and strategies learned over the years. The blog quickly gained a following, attracting readers from all walks of life who were eager to improve their financial knowledge. Through blog posts, webinars, and online courses, Alex extended their reach, empowering even more people to take control of their finances.

Recognizing the importance of community support, Alex joined forces with local organizations to promote financial literacy on a larger scale. They helped organize community events, bringing together financial experts and residents to discuss various topics, from home buying and retirement planning to tax strategies and entrepreneurship.

One of the most rewarding initiatives was a partnership with a non-profit organization that provided financial counseling to low-income families. Alex volunteered their time, offering personalized advice and helping families create realistic financial plans. The gratitude and progress of these families reaffirmed Alex's commitment to making a difference.

As Alex sat in the park, they took a moment to look back on the journey. From the uncertainty and challenges of early adulthood to the confidence and independence they now enjoyed, the transformation had been profound. Each milestone celebrated, each person mentored, and each community event organized was a testament to the power of knowledge, resilience, and the support of a community.

The journey had not only been about achieving financial independence but also about growing as a person, gaining confidence, and finding a sense of purpose in helping others. Alex knew that the adventure was far from over. There would always be new goals to set, new challenges to overcome, and new opportunities to make a positive impact.

With a deep sense of fulfillment and a heart full of gratitude, Alex stood up from the bench, ready to continue the journey. The path ahead was sure to be filled with more learning, growth, and the chance to inspire and empower others.

Conclusion

Alex's journey from financial uncertainty to confidence had been marked by perseverance, continuous learning, and a commitment to helping others. Celebrating milestones like paying off student loans and achieving financial independence was not just about personal success but also about giving back to the community and promoting financial literacy.

As Alex moved forward, they remained dedicated to mentoring others and fostering a culture of financial empowerment. The journey's end was not a conclusion but a new beginning—an opportunity to continue making a difference, one step at a time. With a clear vision and a passionate heart, Alex was ready to face the future, knowing that the best adventures were yet to come.

The Journey's End

1. **Transformation Through Perseverance**:

    - The journey from financial uncertainty to confidence and independence requires perseverance and disciplined financial planning.

    - Each milestone achieved represents significant progress toward financial stability and independence.

2. **Celebrating Milestones**:

    - Paying off student loans symbolized the end of a financial obligation and the beginning of financial freedom.

    - Completing an emergency fund provided a safety net, enabling calculated risks and seizing new opportunities.

3. **Achieving Financial Independence**:

    - Financial independence allows focusing on passions and pursuits without the pressure of financial instability.

    - Careful budgeting, strategic investments, and continuous learning are essential to building a diversified portfolio generating passive income.

4. **Valuable Lessons From Challenges**:

   - Challenges and setbacks teach valuable lessons and strengthen resolve.

   - Overcoming obstacles is part of the journey toward financial success.

5. **Giving Back to the Community**:

   - Mentoring others and promoting financial literacy is a way to give back to the community.

   - Offering workshops and interactive sessions on budgeting, saving, and investing helps lay the groundwork for others' future financial success.

6. **Extending Reach Through Blogging**:

   - Sharing insights and strategies through a financial literacy blog can attract a wide audience.

   - Blog posts, webinars, and online courses empower more people to take control of their finances.

7. **Community Support and Collaboration**:

   - Joining forces with local organizations to promote financial literacy on a larger scale is crucial.

   - Organizing community events and partnering with non-profits to provide financial counseling enhances community impact.

9. **Personal Growth and Fulfillment**:

  - The journey is not only about achieving financial independence but also about personal growth, gaining confidence, and finding purpose in helping others.

  - Mentoring and community involvement provide immense satisfaction and reaffirm commitment to making a difference.

10. **Ongoing Journey**:

  - The journey doesn't end with achieving financial independence; it continues with setting new goals and overcoming new challenges.

  - Continuous learning, growth, and the chance to inspire and empower others keep the journey alive.

11. **Dedication to Financial Empowerment**:

  - Remaining dedicated to mentoring others and fostering a culture of financial empowerment is essential.

  - Each step forward is an opportunity to make a positive impact.

12. **Embracing Future Adventures**:

  - The journey's end is a new beginning, filled with more learning, growth, and opportunities to make a difference.

- With a clear vision and passionate heart, embracing future adventures with confidence ensures continued success.

Chapter 14

The Call to Action

The gymnasium buzzed with the excited chatter of students as they took their seats, eager to hear from the guest speaker. Alex stood at the front, looking out at the young faces full of potential and curiosity. Today, Alex had the opportunity to share their journey and inspire the next generation to take control of their financial futures.

As the last students settled down, the school principal introduced Alex, highlighting their achievements and dedication to financial literacy. The room fell silent as Alex stepped up to the microphone, a sense of purpose and passion evident in their eyes.

"Good morning, everyone," Alex began, their voice resonating with confidence. "I'm thrilled to be here today to talk to you about something that can truly change your life—financial literacy. But first, let me tell you a bit about my journey."

Alex recounted their story, from the uncertainty they faced after graduating college to the financial struggles and setbacks that shaped their path. They spoke about the mentors who had guided them, the workshops and seminars that had expanded their knowledge, and the practical strategies that had helped them achieve financial independence.

"I wasn't always confident about managing money," Alex admitted. "In fact, I made a lot of mistakes early on. But each mistake taught me something valuable, and with every lesson learned, I grew more knowledgeable and more determined."

Alex shared specific lessons that had been pivotal in their journey:

- **The Importance of Budgeting:** "Understanding where your money goes is the first step. Budgeting helps you take control and make informed decisions about your spending."
- **Building an Emergency Fund:** "Life is unpredictable. Having an emergency fund gives you peace of mind and a safety net for those unexpected expenses."
- **Investing for the Future:** "Don't be afraid to invest. Start small, learn the basics, and watch your money grow over time. Compound interest is a powerful tool."
- **Continuous Learning:** "The financial world is always changing. Keep learning, stay informed, and adapt your strategies as needed."

With the foundational lessons shared, Alex shifted the focus to the students, urging them to take the first steps on their own financial journeys.

"Now, I want to talk about you," Alex said, looking directly at the students. "You have the power to shape your future. It's never too early to start thinking about your financial goals and how you're going to achieve them."

Alex encouraged the students to set specific, achievable financial goals, whether it was saving for a new gadget, starting a college fund, or planning for a future business.

"Write down your goals," Alex advised. "Having clear goals will keep you motivated and focused. And don't be afraid to dream big. With the right knowledge and determination, you can achieve anything."

Alex emphasized the importance of taking control of their finances early on. They shared practical tips on how to get started, such as opening a savings account, tracking expenses, and seeking out educational resources.

"Taking control of your finances is empowering," Alex explained. "It gives you the freedom to make choices that align with your values and aspirations. It allows you to build a secure and prosperous future, not just for yourself but for your family and community."

To illustrate the impact of financial literacy, Alex shared stories of individuals who had transformed their lives through smart financial decisions. They talked about a single mother who had built a successful business, a young entrepreneur who had created innovative products, and families who had achieved financial stability and independence.

"These people started just like you, with questions and

uncertainties," Alex said. "But they acted. They learned, they planned, and they persevered. And you can do the same."

Alex encouraged the students to seek out mentors, attend workshops, and use online resources to expand their financial knowledge. They emphasized the importance of community and support, highlighting the benefits of learning from others and sharing experiences.

As the talk neared its conclusion, Alex made a heartfelt call to action.

"Today, I challenge you to take the first step on your financial journey," Alex declared. "Start small, stay curious, and never stop learning. The choices you make today will shape your tomorrow. Take control of your finances, and you'll have the power to build the future you envision."

The room erupted in applause as Alex finished speaking. Students approached Alex afterward, eager to ask questions and share their own financial goals. The energy and enthusiasm in the room were palpable, a testament to the impact of Alex's message.

The Call to Action

1. **Importance of Financial Literacy**:

   - Financial literacy can change lives by empowering individuals to take control of their financial futures.
   - Sharing personal financial journeys and practical strategies can inspire and educate others.

2. **Learning from Mistakes**:

   - Mistakes are valuable learning experiences that can lead to greater financial knowledge and determination.
   - Early financial struggles can shape a more informed and resilient approach to money management.

3. **Essential Financial Principles**:

   - **Budgeting**: Understanding where money goes is crucial for making informed spending decisions.
   - **Emergency Fund**: Having an emergency fund provides peace of mind and a safety net for unexpected expenses.
   - **Investing**: Starting small and learning the basics of investing can lead to significant growth over time through compound interest.

- **Continuous Learning**: The financial world is always changing, so staying informed and adaptable is essential.

4. **Setting and Achieving Financial Goals**:

   - Setting specific, achievable financial goals helps maintain motivation and focus.

   - Writing down goals and dreaming big can drive progress and success.

5. **Taking Control of Finances**:

   - Taking control of finances is empowering and enables individuals to make choices that align with their values and aspirations.

   - Practical steps to get started include opening a savings account, tracking expenses, and seeking educational resources.

6. **Impact of Financial Literacy**:

   - Smart financial decisions can transform lives, leading to successful businesses, innovative products, and financial stability.

   - Real-life examples illustrate the benefits of financial literacy and the potential for positive change.

7. **Seeking Mentors and Community Support**:

   - Seeking out mentors, attending workshops, and using online resources can expand financial knowledge.

- Learning from others and sharing experiences within a community fosters growth and support.

8. **Empowerment Through Action**:

   - Taking the first step on the financial journey is crucial; starting small, staying curious, and committing to continuous learning are key.

   - The choices made today will shape the future, so taking control of finances is essential for building a secure and prosperous future.

9. **Inspiring the Next Generation**:

   - Encouraging young people to start thinking about their financial goals early on can set them on a path to success.

   - Providing practical tips and sharing inspiring stories can motivate them to take action and pursue financial independence.

10. **Building a Financially Literate Community**:

    - Promoting financial literacy within the community helps create a supportive environment for financial growth.

    - Empowering individuals through education and mentorship strengthens the overall financial well-being of the community.

11. Lifelong Commitment to Financial Education:

- Financial literacy is a continuous journey, not a one-time achievement.
- Staying committed to learning and adapting to new financial challenges ensures long-term success.

Conclusion

Addressing the students was a profoundly rewarding experience for Alex. Reflecting on their journey from financial uncertainty to confidence, they felt a deep sense of fulfillment in inspiring others to take control of their financial futures.

The adventure of financial literacy was ongoing, filled with new challenges and opportunities. By sharing their story and empowering the next generation, Alex was contributing to a larger movement of financial education and empowerment.

As they left the school that day, Alex knew that their journey was far from over. There were more people to mentor, more stories to share, and more communities to support. With each step, Alex was not only continuing their own adventure but also helping others embark on theirs, building a brighter, more financially secure future for all.

Made in the USA
Monee, IL
04 November 2026

67387902R00066